The Dragonfly Secret

A Story of Boundless Love

By

Clea Adams and John Adams

Illustrated by

Barbara L. Gibson

Feather Rock Books, Inc.
Maple Plain, Minnesota

A Note from the Authors and Publisher

The Dragonfly Secret: A Story of Boundless Love encourages children and adults to explore life's infinite possibilities. It is a companion book to *The Dragonfly Door*, a children's story about loss and change.

Because young minds are impressionable, we recommend that a parent or other responsible adult read this book first to determine its suitability for individual children.

Published by Feather Rock Books, Inc. – Maple Plain, Minnesota
Text copyright © 2008 by Feather Rock Books, Inc.
Illustrations copyright © 2008 by Feather Rock Books, Inc.

For further information or to comment on this book, please contact us at:
Feather Rock Books, Inc.
P.O. Box 99
Maple Plain, MN 55359

1-877-473-9091

For additional copies of this book, please visit your local bookstore or our website at www.featherrockbooks.com.

Printed in Canada

First Edition
First Printing, 2008

Author photography by Michelle's Portrait Design

Publisher's Cataloging-in-Publication
(Provided by Quality Books, Inc.)

    Adams, Clea.
      The dragonfly secret : a story of boundless love /
   written by Clea Adams and John Adams ; illustrated by
   Barbara L. Gibson. -- 1st ed.
      p. cm.
      SUMMARY: While playing in a garden, Lea, a dragonfly,
   agrees to help a mysterious boy contact his parents,
   ease their grief and give them hope.
    LCCN 2008902727
    ISBN-13: 978-1-934066-13-3
    ISBN-10: 1-934066-13-3

   1. Future life--Juvenile fiction. 2. Death--Juvenile fiction. 3. Dragonflies Juvenile
fiction. [1. Future life--Fiction. 2. Death--Fiction. 3. Dragonflies--Fiction. 4. Insects--
Fiction.]   I. Adams, John, 1960-II. Gibson, Barbara, ill. III. Title.

PZ7.A19835Dra 2008   [E]
     QBI08-600139

To our parents
To Abby, Jeff, Andrew, and Chris – with much love
– *CA and JA*

To my mom
– *BLG*

On a bright summer morning, Lea played hide-and-seek in the garden with Tess, her butterfly friend. She hid among the flowers and giggled to herself. Suddenly, a boy appeared. He sat on the ground next to some daisies and rested his chin in his hands. Lea moved closer to get a better look. He turned toward her and smiled.

"Hi, there, Giggles!" he said. "Don't worry. I won't tell the butterfly where you are."

The air around him was warm, like a hug. Everything near him shone brighter – the grass, the roses, and the daisies. Even the bumblebees seemed more yellow.

"Quick, hide inside there," the boy said, pointing to a hole in the tree next to him.

"Thanks," Lea replied, darting for the tree. "And the name's Lea."

Tess searched the garden while Lea hid. The boy kept her company. His baseball stories made her laugh.

Tess finally found Lea's hiding spot. Soon after, Tess left to go home. Lea waved goodbye but stayed and played tag with the boy.

The late afternoon sun painted the garden purple and red.

"Do you want to meet here again in the morning?" the boy asked.

"I'd like that," Lea said.

The next morning Lea flew across the meadow to the flower garden and landed on the fence. She saw the boy tossing a baseball into the air and expertly catching it with a worn glove.

"Hey, want to play hide-and-seek?" she called out.

"Sure. You hide first." He closed his eyes and began counting to ten.

Again, they played for hours. Evening approached and they rested in the cool grass.

"I had fun today," Lea said. After a moment she softly asked, "How come you haven't told me your name or where you live? And how do you know all the great hiding places around here?"

The boy laughed. "How about I let you in on a secret?"

"Sure," said Lea, her eyes wide. "I love secrets."

"First, I need to ask you to help do something," the boy said. "Is it a deal?"

"Hmm," said Lea. "Will the something be hard to do?"

"Not for you," he replied. The boy paused for a moment and looked up at the soft blue sky. Then he quietly continued, "Listen carefully:

You have a message to deliver,
a promise so true,
it can only be carried by a dragonfly like you."

Lea moved closer to him, fluttering her wings.

"Are you interested?" he asked.

"I think so," Lea said, landing on his glove. "Is this some kind of game?"

"It's more like a puzzle," the boy said. "Tomorrow, I need you to come to the garden again and do three things. If you do, you will discover the secret. Are you in?"

"Yes, of course!" Lea exclaimed. "Tell me the three things."

"First, find a baseball cap in the garden," the boy said. "When you find it, you must land on it and stay there until you see me. Can you promise to do that? You have to promise!"

"Sure, that's easy. I promise," said Lea. "What are the other two things?"

"You will know soon enough," the boy said. "See you tomorrow!"

The boy left the garden, tossing his baseball into the air.

"I'm going to find that baseball cap right now," Lea whispered.

Lea searched through the flowers and trees. She peered behind a large rock and under leaves. An old couple walked along the stone path. They noticed Lea darting back and forth.

The old man smiled and asked, "Are you the dragonfly who is helping a boy – the boy who likes to toss baseballs into the air?"

"Yes," Lea said shyly.

"Have you found the baseball cap?" asked the old woman.

"Not yet, I just started looking for it," Lea replied.

"We are counting on you," the old woman said.

The tenderness in her eyes drew Lea closer. The air around her became warm. The flowers and grass brightened.

There must be something special about these people, Lea thought. She decided to ask, "Do you know what else I'm supposed to do?"

"Yes, of course we do," said the woman. "It's very simple. Tomorrow you must come to this garden and find a brown bear. When you see it, land on it. Don't move from it until you see us. Can you do that? Promise you will!"

"I think so," Lea said.

"You can do it," the old man said gently.

"Okay, I promise. But the boy said there were three things I needed to do to learn the secret," said Lea, feeling a bit flustered. "I only know two, find a baseball cap and then find a bear. What's the third thing I need to do?"

"We cannot tell you," replied the woman.

The old man looked up at the sky for a moment and then quietly said,

"You have a message to deliver,
a promise so true,
it can only be carried by a dragonfly like you."

The couple waved goodbye to Lea and disappeared around a bend in the path.

Puzzled, Lea decided to fly home and get an early start the next day.

In the morning, Lea dashed across the meadow to the garden. On her way, she thought about places to look for the baseball cap and bear.

"I bet the baseball cap is either by the tree swing or the hole in the tree," she said to herself.

When Lea reached the garden, she immediately began her search. She hovered over the swing. Nothing was there.

"Hmm, I'd better check the tree."

She circled the giant oak tree and darted in and out of the hole. She could not find a baseball cap or a bear.

Lea explored other parts of the garden. She looked under a picnic table and peeked inside the gardener's tool shed.

Suddenly, Lea felt a strange stillness. The birds and insects were quiet. Someone nearby was crying. Lea flew cautiously toward the sound.

A woman sat on a wooden bench in the corner of the garden. Lea could see her face wet with tears. The light around the woman seemed dim. For a moment, Lea's wings felt very heavy. She, too, felt sad.

This must be what the woman feels, she thought.

The woman continued to cry. Uncertain of what to do, Lea made her way to the branch of a nearby tree. She looked at the woman. Something caught her attention. Beside the woman on the bench was a baseball cap!

"There it is!" Lea gasped with excitement. "But how can I touch the cap without disturbing that woman? What if I scare her?"

Lea remembered her promise to the boy.

"I have to try," she decided.

Holding her breath, Lea flew slowly toward the woman. Her wings shimmered in the sunlight as she moved closer and closer.

Crack! A snapping twig sent Lea's heart crashing against her chest. She zipped back toward the tree.

"Who is that?" said Lea as a man walked into the garden and sat down beside the woman. He put his arm around her.

The couple held hands and leaned their heads together.

A warm breeze began to blow. The sky brightened. Lea thought she could hear the boy's voice saying,

"You have a message to deliver,
a promise so true,
it can only be carried by a dragonfly like you."

With new purpose, Lea decided to try again. As she flew closer to the couple, the man turned toward the woman. It was then Lea spotted something small and brown sticking out of his jacket pocket.

"Why, that's a toy bear!" Lea squealed with excitement. "I'll land on the cap like I promised and then touch the bear."

Lea flew to the cap and landed on it. Instantly, the boy appeared. He smiled at her. The woman on the bench pointed at Lea.

"Go touch the bear," the boy whispered. He sat down on the swing nearby.

Lea knew the woman was watching her. She gently cupped the air with her wings and settled onto the brown bear. The woman gasped. The old couple from the path appeared next to the boy. They smiled at Lea.

"Thank you," they said. "We knew you could do it."

The woman stood and pointed a trembling finger at Lea. She said, "Did you see that? Oh, look, the dragonfly was on the cap and now it's on the bear."

Lea looked at the boy. "Quick, what's the third thing I must do to learn the secret?"

The boy smiled. "Lea, you just did it. Look at them."

Lea turned to see that the man and woman were staring at her. She was surprised to see them smiling as they brushed away tears. Her heart raced. Her wings felt light. Lea felt some of their sadness disappear.

She flew toward the boy's outstretched hand. "Who do that bear and cap belong to?"

"Those are mine," said the boy.

"We gave them to him," said the old man.

"David, we love you!" the couple from the bench called out.

"So, your name is David!" Lea exclaimed to the boy.

"Yes," said David.

"They can't see you, can they?" asked Lea.

"No. They have not seen me for a long time," David whispered.

"Who are they?"

"That's my mom and dad," David replied.

David's face filled with love as he joined hands with the old man and old woman.

"And we are David's grandparents," the old woman said proudly.

"Mom, Dad, we miss you too," the man from the bench called out.

"I think I know the secret now," Lea exclaimed. "You are here but only I can see you!"

"That's right!" the boy said.

"So, David, the third thing I had to do was deliver a message from you to your parents, to let them know you are okay and thinking about them."

"Right again," David replied.

"I bet I can help others like you," Lea said. She was eager to carry another message.

"I think you're right," David's grandfather replied. "You have a special gift."

"More like a secret. A dragonfly secret," Lea smiled. "Thanks for picking me, David."

"We picked each other," David said with a grin.

"It's time for us to go," David's grandfather said.

With a wave, David and his grandparents turned and disappeared.

Lea looked at David's mom and dad. They still sat on the bench. His mom's head rested on his dad's shoulder.

Lea flew to them and, for a moment, lingered quietly on the baseball cap.

"Thank you, little dragonfly," they whispered.

The End